A preliminary sketch for a portrait bust of Frank Prewett by Vivienne
Jenkins. Christmas 1957

☞ **Owing to the great demand for this Book,
you are earnestly requested to return it
as soon as read, and on no account to retain it more
than Seven days.**

Reader's No.	Date Due	Reader's No.	Date Due	Reader's No.	Date Due

THE COLLECTED POEMS
OF FRANK PREWETT

THE
COLLECTED
POEMS OF
FRANK
PREWETT

CASSELL · LONDON

CASSELL & COMPANY LTD
35 Red Lion Square, London WC1
MELBOURNE, SYDNEY, TORONTO,
JOHANNESBURG, CAPE TOWN, AUCKLAND

Printed in Great Britain by
The Camelot Press Ltd., London and Southampton
F. 764

CONTENTS

The publishers make acknowledgement to Mrs Dorothy Prewett for permission to print the three broadcast talks, and also to Messrs Heinemann for permission to reprint the three poems from *A Rural Scene*.

INTRODUCTION
by
Robert Graves

Frank Prewett was born in 1893 on his grandfather's Old Ontario farm, and brought up as a strict Protestant. Three broadcast talks about his childhood are printed at the close of this book. Though he does not mention the strain of Iroquois blood in his mother's family, it was manifest in his high cheek-bones, dark colouring, graceful walk, and fiery heart. From school at Toronto, he won an exhibition to Christ Church, Oxford, just before the First World War. He then joined the Royal Artillery; first serving as a battery officer, later in trench mortars, and finally as a staff officer. He was seriously wounded under shell fire and invalided out in 1917. He returned to Oxford, took his degree, and married an English girl.

I met him in 1920, while he was farming near Oxford, and at the same time lecturing at the University School of Agriculture and Forestry. He had privately published a small pamphlet of poems with the Hogarth Press, Richmond, sent me by Siegfried Sassoon. Three of these stuck in my memory, and despite my disappointment with A Rural Scene (Heinemann, 1924), another small collection too often influenced by the facile Georgian style then in vogue, I still reckoned him among the few true poets. In 1926 we both left Oxford and lost touch. I saw no poems of his published anywhere, and concluded that he had gone back to farm in Canada. Nor did any news reach me of him until 1962. Apparently the farm had failed, his marriage had gone wrong, and he drifted about England

vii

*until the Second World War broke out. He then married
again, and joined a bomb-disposal squad at Birmingham
during the Blitz. Later he was employed in operational
research at H.Q. Fighter Command, and sent as adviser
to the Supreme Command in South-East Asia. After the
war, he continued working at the Air Ministry and
H.Q. Technical Training Command. In 1954, he retired
because of ill health to a Cotswold cottage, where he
struggled against pain and decrepitude, working the
land and writing poems. On 16 February 1962 he died at
Raigmore Hospital, Inverness, after a Christmas visit to a
Scottish friend.*

*A few days before this I had been sent a package of
his unpublished poems by Mary Allan, an Air Ministry
colleague to whom he had bequeathed them. She was able
to assure him, before he finally lost consciousness, that I
would get them published at all costs, as a matter of poetic
duty. We have chosen those which seem most characteristic-
ally his. They have, as he wrote to Dr Allan, 'a hard but
true music, and do not belong to the cant of the age.' He
had felt it his duty to write at the orders of the daemon
who rode him, and to see that the poems were presented
in a few copies at least, against the time when 'this cant
has dissolved, and their originality can be accepted by
numbers of men.' His daemon, he explained, had told
him to attempt the simple beyond simplicity, the sensuous
beyond sense, the disdainment of mere fact.*

*'Listen to the rhythms of a storm in the trees! . . . These
poems are my only and true wealth . . . I think I shall
do no more.'*

*Dedicated poets like Frank Prewett are few in any
age; and lamentably so in this.*

R. G.

DEYÁ
MALLORCA

Come Girl, and Embrace

Come girl, and embrace
And ask no more I wed thee;
Know then you are sweet of face,
Soft limbed and fashioned lovingly—
Must you go marketing your charms
In cunning woman-like,
And filled with old wives' tales' alarms?

I tell you, girl, come embrace;
What reck we of churchling and priest
With hands on paunch and chubby face?
Behold, we are life's pitiful least,
And we perish at the first smell
Of death, whither heaves earth
To spurn us cringing into hell.

Come girl, and embrace;
Nay, cry not, poor wretch, nor plead,
But haste, for life strikes a swift pace
And I burn with envious greed:
Know you not, fool, we are the mock
Of gods, time, clothes, and priests?
But come, there is no time for talk.

Met ye my love?
Ye might in France have met him;
He has a wooing smile,
Who sees cannot forget him!
Met ye my Love?—
—We shared full many a mile.

Saw ye my love?
In lands far-off he has been,
With his yellow-tinted hair,
In Egypt such ye have seen,
Ye knew my love?—
—I was his brother there.

Heard ye my love?
My love ye must have heard,
For his voice when he will
Tinkles like cry of bird;
Heard ye my love?—
—We sang on a Grecian hill.

Behold your love,
And how shall I forget him,
His smile, his hair, his song?
Alas, no maid shall get him
For all her love,
Where he sleeps a million strong.

I Went Out Into the Fields

I went out into the fields
In my anguish of mind,
And sought comfort of the trees
For they looked to be kind.

'Alas!' cried they, 'who have peace?—
We are prey that is caught,
The sun warms us, the blast chills,
And we understand not.'

On rolled the world with fools' noise,
But I strode in tears' wrack,
Would God, fools, I too were fool,
Or had light that I lack.

I held the fields all day,
I, a madman, too;
My spirit called aloud
To sift the false from true.

The troubled sun turned black,
Earth heaved to and fro,
Whene'er I spurned the flowers
Lifting heads to grow.

Trees reached their hands to stay,
Whistled birds to me,
'Spurn one, thou spurnest all,
Brother, let things be.

'For not their heads alone
Bleed, but the stars fade
And all things grieve, for we
One fabric are made.'

The heavens and earth do meet
And all things are true,
So trample ye no flowers
Lest skies lose their blue.

The Red-Man

From wilderness remote he breaks
With stealthy springing tread,
And in the town a vision makes
Of time and manners dead.

He scorns to see the things we own,
And steadfast stares beyond,
Alone, impassive, cold, unknown;
With us he feels no bond.

The townsfolk nudging line the street
To see a red-man pass;
They feel ashamed of toil and heat,
And dream of springs and grass.

They see a breathless dusty town
They had not known before;
The red-man in his robes is gone,
The townsfolk toil once more.

And whence he came, and whither fled,
And why, is all unknown;
His ways are strange, his skin is red,
Our ways and skins our own.

Seeing my love but lately come,
And unexpecting she should be found,
I trembled, I was dumb,
And fell upon the ground;
Her only thus in distance to see
Was to me pain so profound
I fell down in an agony.

Oh, who is he often has told
What joy in his love he had,
Or, he never loved, but grew old
Indulging fancy or fad
No more than to tease desire
Or make him romantical sad,
But his heart never shrunk in the fire.

Oh, she does not know what possess,
What despairs ride me every day;
For her vexed, or in slight distress
I am mad, I must fly away,
Or the whole world crack with my rage
And scatter it out of her way,
But she cannot know, or assuage.

Oh, now I see why true love is pale
With no desire but he should die;
Most willing lips are no avail
For not all this is, will satisfy;
Its limit mind cannot entertain,
Love like a madness is for wide and high,
And weep would, though it all might gain.

If Dead, Free

When the last melancholy of my brain,
The final groan, left me faint and bleeding,
I then substanceless and vain,
Only relief, not disaster, heeding,
Had such joy as a man who has lost
A limb that long pained him,
Mirth, hollow-sounding, and crossed
With an in-burning pleading.

But I laughed and knew, if dead
I was free, and the bold sun shining
And the burly wind wrapping my head
Made brighter my peace after repining:
I will think no more of it, I cried,
But if I think not of her, what thought
Have I, whose utter self died
When love died, to limbo resigning?

A Woman's Safety

With his strong hand he drew me up the bank;
I had stumbled but for his hand
Which enclosed all of me safely;
I nestle in him warm and bland.
By the light in our eyes they knew that we loved,
They knew, else I had cried to them:
'I am enclosed in his hand that loves me
Yet I am the more strong to be free.'

We went our separate ways on the heath,
We were all the while clasped together.
We felt a hate so to lose ourselves in the other,
And studied the heather bells for better pleasure.
'Come here,' he cried, 'see as I see,
Hear as I hear! You have not the will
To feel other than I feel the sensibility
Of sun and shower. You must always walk with me.'

But I rustled forward through the cotton grass,
Through the heather bristle. I must be away
From the hand that enclosed me whole
And ended my life though I lived an age and a day.

The Girl Near the Billet

As I ran from my billet at dusk
To join the trudge to our observer post,
She stood before me plump and busk.
I knew her not, yet I knew her most.

We clasped together, we merged our natural joy—
It is more than thirty years, but it is today.
A surging of innocence without alloy
As we unclasped and I took my fearful way.

If I might have stayed a minute long
We had given all to each without thought,
Without jarring intrusion of tongue
And would each have given what is vainly sought.

Often and unexpected, still she comes to me:
Again I join the troop, she trembling stands,
Again our instinct makes us unity,
Again I leave her a kiss on her hands.

Seeking Perfect

Who is this plodding, seeking the perfect true,
Seeker seeking perfect wherever it may lie
Whether in glade still-winter, whether in summer blue,
Seeks knowing it is, and must be his, ere he die.

Poor he shall stay who seeks the lovely, the best,
Condemned to hunger, he the most in gold;
For he carries a gem other jewels to test,
When the perfect he seeks he finds and is bold.

He offers his gem, the seeker to the fairest fair,
To his sensing will be nearest, gentle and kind,
To a woman. He hangs his gem in her hair
And they seek together what perfect they may find.

It is well, this is well, seeker has done well.
Of all her love his woman gives him fill
And soothes his rage. Better in happy hunger dwell
In his fret, so he be seeker still.

Yet Still She Would Stay

We left the road, crossed a sward by a stile
Through a beech copse into the other world:
I warned her this was enchanted ground,
Yet she would lie upon it and remain.

'We have come no more than a mile
But we are leaving the world by a league
Each moment we dare the spell to be here.'
Still she had no fear and would stay.

'What you had is fading instantly away,
While you lie upon the enchanted ground
Our path is grown over, it is late to win back.'
Yet she stretched there and would remain.

'Music and companionable lights,
The bustling pavement, laughter, all you forgo
For the silences of wood and vale.'
Yet she felt in company and would stay.

'It is not always sunshine here and soft air,
And no friend can follow at need
When you have grown hungry and cold.'
But she felt that as nothing and must remain.

'It is sweet, I know how sweet in the obliterate,
To leave the road and thread the copse
And be light of mind, for so you yield your life.'
Yet she was blinded and stubborn and would stay.

I Stared at the Dead

When I awoke I had slept brief,
I waked to strangling of heart,
And I stood attempting new belief
That I thought, yet, was life apart.

I stood and stared at me dead:
Well folded my hands on my breast,
My stretch easy as in my bed,
And I grew troubled at my quest.

This is death before death, desire
Is now, I may know how to die
Before dying and at last acquire
News for all doomed ignorantly.

But while I stood I was seized
And forced into the body on the bed
With hardly a glimpse appeased
Of my soul when I had been dead.

Do Not Go Away So High

You are the sun and the pencilled shade,
You are the glow on the hedgebank elm in May:
The first human heart was made
That we might join together this day.

I bask in the sun and the rippled breeze,
On the open earth is all my bliss,
Where the sunlight searches for gaps in the trees
And all our being for ever is a kiss.

You go up among the moon and the stars
I cannot follow where the stars are shaken,
I cannot follow but lie in the starlight bars
Crying despair of infant feared forsaken.

Do not go away so often or so high
Into the cold spaces where you are alone.
When you are there you can still hear my cry
And come down and be gentle and atone.

In London or in any town
I know not how the wind blows,
Whether from frozen moor or genial down,
But that I am cold or warm it goes.

The rain pelts me, or a thick heat
Hangs on me where I fare.
I see unseeing the parallel of street
That pinches to a wedge afar.

When I am in the country it means much
Where the wind lies, what its tone:
Whether hot or cold to the touch
It is natural to my bone.

A day and a night be and bear with me,
Cling us close together for so long.
In a day and a night all is that can be
Cling we close and each to each belong.

Of such communion comes no satiety
But sweet freshening of mind and heart:
To melt, to nourish, nothing to deny
Taken and given unquestioning who part.

Like reedy bird in treetop tuft unseen
They parting fade who never shall away.
The song in the recess and thicket-screen
Enters the heart elusive. Go, yet elusive stay.

I shall tell you how singing silences are made
And colour from the light and air,
And carry you the distances of light and shade:
All that is loving and sad we shall share.

Hear with me the breeze suffuse the leaves
Behind, below the reedy bird in her green light.
A day and a night the bared heart joys and grieves.
Cling to me openheart a day and night.

Invade Me, Love

Invade me love, longer besieged
I am irresolute, I fear.
I prize the privacy alleged
Than love to be more dear.

You need but mock at my defence
To scatter me and lay me bare:
But when you reason, my pretence
Is armed to know the lack we share.

Love has no kindred in the brain,
Love is the flush of skin, the kiss.
Your pose of thought is my disdain;
In your ardour is my bliss.

Air Raid Warning

The siren howls, the busy harvest gang
Straighten, and shade their eyes. The birds that sang
Fall still, and silent earth and air combine,
Stook and copse moveless. The last siren whine
Splutters in colic pain. The village cur
Yelps and slinks to his lair. In a whir
Women snatch the wash from the line, scold the child,
Slam the door tight. Birds in flighting wild
Flock field to hedge, peer out and twitter soft.
Peke lionheart stands braced in street, flag aloft.
He thrusts his muzzle, he growls from his core
As the faint throbbing, quickening to a roar,
Shakes the senses, assaults the mind
As if the solid earth were undermined.
The old gander claps his wings, his flock arraigns;
His hiss pierces the tumult of the planes:
Unseen in sultry glare, peril and fear
Recede to silence. Trumpet-triumph clear
The siren shouts her joy. Peke lionheart
Spurns the turf. Old gander fiercely apart
Drills his goose-gosling muster. Then start
And intertwine many songs from hides of leaves,
Again the harvest gang draw to the rick with sheaves.

Girl Among Bombs

Birmingham barrack-bulk and smoky stack
Bulges against the westering sheet
Of snow red-sooted in the sunfall track
To clang of tram, swift sibilant of feet.

Where do you go, little one, whither mince your pace
In your shiny hose and paper shoes?
Our hearths are many and your baby face
Will no hearth of a harsh town refuse.

Hurry, hasten, looms a night of shame,
Soon the throbbing peril beats you down.
Hide your eyes, hide your head, from flame;
Stop your ears to rushing shell and bomb.

'I think a person is silly who hides,
And while the shafts hum and our lathes whir round
We don't heed the bombs, and besides
I would rather be busy than mope underground.

'The raids make us excited and we sing
We sing at our lathes, we jig, we sway,
And breast to breast an instant cling,
For when we work close together we are gay.'

Hush, child, cease your song, your arms unbind.
Bombs are war and death. I don't know about war
But the raids make us loving and kind
And eager to share ourselves more than before.

Blackbird

Blackbird by pondered phrase
Talks in the eve of dusk,
In pale trembling sun when fails
The north which breathed all day,
And the lamb clouds melt to blue.
Blackbird from wintered elm
Deliberate and calm
Studies each phrase,
Each phrase for a full song.
Tongues of evening fire
Lick the elm top where he sings,
Where he quickens his phrase
And ruffles and arches and swells
And strides a pace on the black bough,
Clear fluting to me below
In the brief cold fiery dusk.

The Cloud Snake

As I came at dusk to the hump of the wold
I must cross in the sun's afterglow,
A black snake of cloud stretched itself on the ridge
And I was afraid to brave it for the valley below.

Beyond lay the lighted lowland where I would be,
And lighted behind me was the sister vale:
Dark only the ridge under the snake of cloud
And cold the subtle east wind at its tail.

My shelter lies in the moonlight beyond,
I am not daunted by a snake of black.
So I run onward, so runs the cloud before,
Trailing the frosted east wind in her track.

The blue stars dance before me and behind,
Beneath them I know the east wind is not cold.
Do not freeze and fear me on this height,
I seek only to pass from vale to vale of the wold.

The Captive Bird

Love, what a joy it is to tempt,
To lure the wild bird to the ground.
But tame and soon of preen unkempt
The captive bird of love is found.

The roving mind of man is fired
To seek new images, a new fate:
The glowing wings of the desired
She folds when she has won a mate.

Marriage of kindred sense and thought
In man and woman none may find:
In the first rapture to be caught
They are estranged who closest bind.

Randall Is Dead

Randall is dead, Randall lusty and big,
Hard-riding Randall, wise in the ways of the wild,
Who jibbed at books like his mare smelling a pig,
His mare that flung him, his mare more dear than child.

Love of all living blazed from him around:
He cheered the stranger, warmed the poor and cold—
All but his meagre wife who envious frowned,
And his seven-year boy in studying grown old.

When Randall galloped his fields a mile away,
He dwarfed the trees, as the sun he shone.
Maid or man he smote hard by his death this day;
Our fields must be barren now great Randall has gone.

He lies in the dust, bronze and tawny as in life,
And his loved mare peevishly snatches the grass
Waiting his mounting and their joyful strife;
But his strength is stretched in the dust whoever may pass.

Naked Overlong

Earth, tree, hedge, you have been naked overlong,
Too imitating woman thinking pinions best—
Yet she has long time of beauty to be dressed,
And yours like hers is beauty sparse, sinuous and strong
In nakedness, when I would have you rounded
And in green and sheeny firmness bounded.

You delight me always, trees, but have you not seen
The windflowers blowing at your feet,
The mosses emerald and firm where I have my seat,
And the bluebells streaking purple on their green?
The new grass is thrusting the old bents aside,
Even the shrubs of the hedge wear a green pride.

You may say you stay bare for the flowers' good
So they may bloom and seed in the light
As a woman be bonny not for hers but her man's delight.
But I know you indulge an ascetic mood
And neither of you care that I long for luxuriance,
For colour, fullness. I weary of artistic durance.

The Opening of the Land

Now from black hedge and cloggy dike
The countryman, billhook and axe laid by
In the first genial sun, with share and spike
Opens the sallow ploughland to the sky.

The fragrant fields to the distant down he sees
Bright with sky in the blue April haze,
Lost villages and farms in clumps of trees
And the first cattle from the yards at graze.

At this season like the migrant birds
His heart out-flutters to the northern skies
To plains where the red horseman wheels his herds
Or the squat Mongol ice and water plies.

But the plough calls, the master plough
To sow the winter-sallowed fields:
No dream but harvest dreaming now—
Soft sun and shower, abundant yields.

I Went a Mile

I went a mile, a mile no more than long,
And a lurcher dog accompanied me:
The larks fluttered their wingbeat song
And slid from air to earth intermittently
While the dog-fool snuffed the banks along.

It was chill from the east, yet the trees
Were leaf-laden and spring-grown,
And though I could not view them at ease
The garden flowers were fully blown
And bent to the subtle breath of the breeze.

The May month as fair is as unkind;
I am cold, too cold to love your good.
The dog is hot with smells he cannot find
Though I prod him into the deeps of the wood
And I to your beauty am perversely blind.

Sleeping Apart

Though it is dark night and we are apart,
I know that you weep;
And when you are restless in heart
Neither of us can sleep.

I do not weep because I am sad
Or because of lonely fears.
My fullness of heart makes me glad
And overflows into tears.

When we part we lie the more close,
More twined of soul.
Love in our limbs is gross,
Loving in lust is not whole.

That is babble, for if you were right
We would not now be awake:
When we are mingled in breath and sight
Then we sleep and fret forsake.

Hated by Stars

I am pressed down by the stars;
They are far off yet they press me down.
I would have a roof over me laced with bars.
I am too small to bear their frown.

A speck and a speck and other specks whirl apart
In lighted cold, colder for light:
In their mists is no home for a heart,
Only so to be daunted and in fright.

Now a field of grass is cold
In the first of March when daisies shine
Like the stars, but those sky stars are bold
And they hate me for heat that is mine.

Go Your Way

Love has been, love is not;
Go each our ways.
Inquisitorial thought
Only a wraith would raise.

We, who cannot submit
A tittle of our pride,
For mating are unfit:
Brain is a barren bride.

Yet you are lovely still
And will be though we part.
Go your way, let your will
Be greater than your heart.

Not all honour is in mind;
The intellect's embrace
Is not in full refined,
Nor passion all disgrace.

The Pack

I lay dear treasure for you,
I have no treasure that I bear on my back,
Yet I lay riches in your view
Do not doubt me by the smallness of my pack.

All that I have I, delighted, bestow.
I lay it down, I spread it with care
At your feet: approve my show
It is the all of all love that lies there.

Braggart no more, I am grown wise.
I recline, I not resist your lies.
Your beauty as your love is cold
Whether you insinuate or scold.

Excitedly I voyaged home to you
After long away, hoping that you too
Would be happy at my return
And our loving would relearn.

Release me now from board and bed,
Let your mean hunger be by other fed
Where resurgent adolescence takes to wit
To brighten middle age. I am bored with it.

To Death

Death help me accommodate my will,
Make yourself loved that I loathe,
Dull me to think of earthen grave,
Fire and sea spare me. Need me
To think no more, or to love as a bed
The wet consuming dark and chilly earth,
This mind and feel to cease to be,
To hear no fluttering leaf,
But lie all time in moveless apathy.

Can I Bind a Bud?

Once more I hear Creation's apophthegm
The fevered hastening grass proclaiming
Through cemented sodden clay by frail stem;
I crush at a touch mastery beyond maiming.

What power can cease birds' nest and flourish
To dash in my face if I force their thicket hiding?
Not spitting hail or drought can lack their nourish
Though they die, creative live, force deriding.

Can I bind a bud to cease its swelling,
Or by a stone confine a tree's rooting?
Though all combine to make repelling
Yet Creation continues indestructible fruiting.

Rain Descends

June with oppressive air long threatening rain
Hot leafy season, the birds rendered mute,
Dried up the ponds, scorched the shadeless plain,
Limp hung the elm, drought in his deep root.

The gaunt husbandman sees in pasture dry
His cattle, head hung, cluster under hedge,
The dust across his withered mangolds fly,
His dusty wheat stand thin with flagging fledge.

Then a thin haze spreads on the glaring sun
The limp leaves flap in a cooler air,
The old sows in the orchard run
Bearing straw in their jaws for a dry lair.

Then the rain slowly from the hill
Descends on the plain and lays the dust.
The husbandman under an oak sees the rain spill
And earth open her bosom with an eager lust.

Sun, eager life's maker, too eager sun;
Rain, life's nurture, soothing healing rain.
The cattle feeding move from the hedge as one,
The corn new washed glistens and blooms again.

The Soldier

My years I counted twenty-one
Mostly at tail of plough:
The furrow that I drove is done,
To sleep in furrow now.

I leapt from living to the dead
A bullet was my bane.
It split this nutshell rind of head,
This kernel of a brain.

A lad to life has paid his debts
Who bests and kills his foe,
And man upon his sweetheart gets,
To reap as well as sow.

But I shall take no son by hand,
No greybeard bravo be:
My ghost is tethered in the sand
Afar from my degree.

The Birch Tree

I walk on the hill, the hill higher than the heath.
It is a mountain to the vale below.
There is nothing on the sour sand of the hill
But myself and a birch tree in blow
Of breeze, nodding as it nodding will,
Be it man or a great lizard a million years ago.

The sour sand made the beauty here,
Made the uncomfortable village where it lies
In the valley, made the beautiful birch
Not for your eyes or my eyes,
Or any eyes, or any present smirch,
But to be God's beauty's assize.

What if man move at beauty, what if at thought?
It is but reflection, what has always been:
No origin in him that he may arrogate.
The birch was graceful before it was seen,
The breeze was the breeze of the first fate
Of mind universal and serene.

If I walk always, if I humbly wait
Please, if I try, may I know what may be known.
I gladly dare to be sense of sense and mind.
But tell me: before me, was the birch alone
Or was it visited by love as kind
Of lizard, bird, as mammal to man grown?

Can it be lovely if not lovely known?
Has the trembling of the birch made me see
That birch is beautiful, or had it beauty then
When the great lizard was all to be,
And man skulked small in jungle fen?
Did he know his beauty's destiny?

You Use Me With Dread

The bunching hare lazily raises her ears
Lip-lops a pace, nibbles her breast,
Plucks at the clover: then she hears
And knows and leaps in tussock pressed.

The mole deviously ripples the ground.
Insensate in her hunt, she opens her track;
Her trembling snout sniffs all around
And in caverned castle she plunges back.

From the rushes the moorhen glides,
Turning forward her black bead of eye
On me, and fades to shadow where she hides
Her floated clutch covered and dry.

May I not walk this bank where I was bred,
Have I no right of the life which you bear:
I harm not, yet you use me with dread
Who ask of you no other than to share.

I Shall Take You in Rough Weather

I shall take you in rough weather
Where veering wind knows not to cease or settle,
Where December pine on blue and white tosses his feather.
Once you are out of doors the tang is good mettle.

When storms rage and filter under door,
Without you when the house rocks I am afraid.
Infinitude of enmity and cold and unbearable more
The loneliness within walls than in the glade.

We shall warm each other in the lee of trees
Where gale is hushed, where no obstinate wall
Angers the gale, where elemental enmities
For small creatures and lovers are musical.

If I Love You

If I love you, do I prize
What is your mind?
Am I dazzled by your eyes,
Which are grey and kind?

If I love you, do I know
That I doubt your breed,
That alone is best to go,
That your loving is your greed?

But better live than die
Until potency is dead:
Best at your feet to lie
Nor live whence life has fled.

My Bride is Battle

Oh why do you groan, restless soldier boy?
Is it for your white bride, is she your only joy?
I am as cool and as the nightfall fair.
My arms are soft and heavy sleek my hair.

Oh my bride is neither white nor black,
Nor plump nor thin, yet lover I not lack:
Her clamorous cosseting I in revolt deny,
Yet love for her I cannot satisfy.

My bride is battle, she me comforts deep,
She after tumult comforts me asleep;
Her iron front feeds me with fire,
I die, but battle is my all desire.

Plea for Peace

A steep valley overhung by trees
And a ditch ripple, noiseless, nosing its way
Where dwell all seasons quiet and at ease,
Nor bird nor shine but comforting peace all day.

Let the plain be bare, wide and lone
That hides the valley, the noiseless rill:
Brack be the water, slippery the stone
So there be peace, peace and quiet still.

Cold Loving

Cotswold from Ceylon

Ash and elder, maple and thorn
To grey longwinter wold belong:
Ash last-leafen, first leaf-fallen
Most shows delicate in wold summer-sullen.

No yielding lover you, slowly lovely seen:
Your love is ask of frost, of northing keen,
Long-tarried spring, defeated flowers:
Brazen the loving once was ours.

I in this tropic richness where abound
Sweet waters and the palm, more fond
Would wold-faithful afar choose be there
And ash and elder and the thorn be bare.

Rooks

Cawing rooks, crying cawing doom
For stubbles overturned where you last meagre fed,
Home now to elm tops, hungry home,
The cold east and north winds wed.

Feed on past plenty and again devise
To strew a harvest where the prudent glean.
Ride next year's rainbow when this year's dies,
Plump out with feathers, laugh though you are lean.

The Void Between

Of shattered youth the reliquary
Is still to seek, still hope to find.
Dawn grows insidiously strong.
The damned chiefly desire to be saved.
Man in woman seeks lost innocence;
Woman in man her lost child.
Though we cling together we are isolate
And reach vainly to close the void between.

The Warm Smiling Sun

Rain scoured the hills to rocky courses,
Fire heaved up mountains through the sea,
Man was prostrate and undone.
Then swept over waste the three swift horses
Of the charioted calm deity,
The warm smiling sun.

Two Songs of Love

I

Rhyme me a riddle:
Black night breathes softly,
Breathes love softly for your love of me.
Brief abiding, be a while
First winter day discarding leaves
Ash leaves, how they cling, how they clown
As they fall in radiant sun
After white-frost night they twirl down
Bride night in battle raid.
Nor do I condemn war
Which brought me you.

II

Consume me with love.
I am consumed
For a while, for all while
To seek the heights, the deeps,
The distances of mind,
Our pagan joy.
No locking of our glance,
Love imagined,
Foolishly facile,
Garrulous and credulous,
Amorous, then ascetic religious.
Better laugh than weep
The felt-afar pulse of the sea.
Butterfly flaunts only grubs to bring
That is her end, not her dazzle of wing.

Three Broadcast Talks (*1954*)

FARM LIFE IN ONTARIO
FIFTY YEARS AGO

I

The community where I was born was mostly of English descent. Their forebears of the eighteenth century had been trappers who, as fur-bearing animals became scarce, began to depend upon cultivated land. They occupied this land where and as they liked, if they were on good terms with the Iroquois Indians, who were then a powerful nation. The log cabin of the trapping days became the centre of a clearing where they sowed wheat, maize, barley and potatoes. At first, like the early trappers, they used the rivers as highways, but gradually clearings were linked by trails which grew into roads, corduroy roads. A corduroy road consisted of cedar logs laid side by side across it. Road maintenance was by throwing down more cedar logs from the limitless forest through which the road was no more than a ribbon. Corduroy is very bumpy to travel upon.

These were the pioneers, the men who subdued the forest by the axe and fed themselves by the hoe. Each man by himself, with only an ox to help him, prised out tree stumps and glacial boulders and sledged them to the boundaries of his fields. In the winter the pioneers trapped game and shot wildfowl. During the first few years they sold nothing and bought nothing. They clothed themselves in skins. On stormy snow-bound winter days when they could not fell the forest, they made tables and chairs and chests of drawers. When at last a man had crops to sell, he bought himself a cow in calf and a farrowing sow, and then he got himself a wife. The settlers would probably have to go as far as Toronto, eighty miles away, to look for wives. It was in Toronto that the Loyalists had gathered who refused to be citizens of the new-fangled United States of America.

From these beginnings it was my lot to be born on a large and fertile farm. The farmhouse was of cream-coloured brick, and set in the middle of the main part of the farm, about half a mile from the road which, being a military highway, was well-paved. Only its lesser side-turnings were still of corduroy. The drive from road to farmhouse was lined by sugar maple trees. The fields nearest the highway were square, each about twenty acres, and as clean and tidy as a cottage garden. Behind these were similar square fields but with boulders scattered upon them. Still further back the fields were thick with tree stumps as well as boulders. Every field was cultivated, but the stump and boulder-strewn fields were ploughed and sown scratchily. Every spare hour was given to clearing these stumps and boulders. Four generations had laboured at it and the work was not yet done.

Beyond the cultivation lay a woodland of some eighty acres of pure maple sugar growth. The sugar maple is a dull tree of the size and character of sycamore. This woodland was cared for with as much solicitude as the show fields along the highway. All undergrowth had been cleared. The oak, elm and hickory trees, and the fine-leaved maples whose leaves turn red and gold in autumn, had been felled. My grandfather had planted young sugar maples in their places. A sugar maple takes about twenty-five to thirty years to become productive, for trees mature slowly in the brief summers of Ontario. But my grandfather was that sort of man. When he was seventy he set out an apple orchard of twenty acres. His neighbours teased him about it, yet he lived to see the orchard in full bearing.

On top of the farmhouse kitchen was a large bell which was rung in a series of slow strokes to let the men in the fields know that their food would be ready in a quarter of an hour, or in a rapid clanging to warn them of trouble, which might be fire—most grievous of all calamities, or merely that the bull was loose, snorting and tearing up the turf outside the kitchen window.

The barn was in front of the house at about one hundred yards' distance. It was a huge yet harmonious building of wood, painted red. The pillars of squared oak and the great beams on the roof gave it the atmosphere of a church inside. The winters are so cold in Ontario, and so full of snow, that all the stock and crops must be brought under a roof. I remember the building of the barn. The stone foundations had been made during the previous summer. The pillars of the barn were oak trees squared by adze. The squared logs were brought to the barn site by log rollers, and there the holes were gouged in them which would hold the cross beams and rafters. Wooden pegs were fashioned in thousands to bind the timbers together. Not a nail was used in the whole barn, except in the boards forming the roof and wall covering. It took two men a whole winter to saw these boards out of elm logs. Neither architect nor builder was employed in the making of the barn, yet every beam fitted exactly into every other and the balanced symmetry of the barn is a pleasure to look at to this day.

When all the timbers were ready and the harvest had been got, neighbours from far and near were invited to our Barn Bee. In three days the structure of the barn was complete. It remained only to fix the wall and roof boards. Everyone at the barn-raising ate and drank hugely and was boisterously happy. My sister and I, who had been watching the raising of the beams by crane while they swayed crazily until a man aloft seized an end and worked it into its socket and pinned it were, in our turn, tied round our middles and hoisted aloft, where we were heartily spanked, hardly knowing whether to laugh or cry, and very frightened at spinning in mid-air. Horse-play was the favourite humour of our family and neighbours.

Now, these Ontario farmers of fifty years ago were peasants. To be a peasant is to have a particular way of regarding life. It is a state of mind. A man can be a peasant equally whether he is rich or poor, lettered or unlettered. A peasant is a man who is the slave of his land and loves his servitude. He could not have felt otherwise after four generations of making a farm and a home out of the wilderness. His experiences made him suspicious of change and determined of principle. No intellectual brilliance or appreciation of the arts would have turned forest and marsh into rich farmland and a stable society. From the very beginning the pioneers kept public order. On our own farm a court of pioneers had met to try a highwayman. He had a fair hearing, was convicted, and immediately hanged in a grove of trees which my sister and I often visited, fascinated yet nervous that the hanged man might appear before us. There was the stone which marked his grave, the same slim slab as for other burials, but uninscribed.

My grandfather was strict in a puritan religious observance, as were all other of our farmer neighbours. We said grace at every meal, and prayers were held in the kitchen every morning before breakfast, which the whole family and the farm servants attended. With deliberation and gravity my grandfather read a chapter from the family Bible, nearly always from the Old Testament where God was given to anger and threats of vengeance. We children listened apathetically. It was clear that too few could be admitted to Heaven to include us, and our sins had been many times enlarged upon by our elders and our doom foretold. Then we all knelt at our chairs while my grandfather prayed. He prayed at length, eloquently and passionately, that we might do God's will and be upright in all our dealings, and be duly rewarded for our merit in the world to come. When the prayer was ended we all said 'Amen' loudly and leapt into our chairs, clamouring for breakfast.

During haying and harvest we would have working for us an Irishman and some of the endless succession of his daughters. This Irishman had squatted on a detached part of our farm and established his title to a log cabin, a barn, and twenty acres of good land. His wife and daughters did the farming for him. He could shoot a black bear in autumn when bears are fat. He had trout and bass fishing. He snared squirrels and marmots. He made cider, so did every farmer, but he also ran a still, and for this he was shunned and despised.

We children were forbidden to speak to the Irishman, but one of our favourite playgrounds was a tract of moorland, and the way to it passed his cottage. He always seemed to be at hand when we went that way: tall, unshaven and happy. He would address us noisily in the most friendly way, inviting the darlings to enter his poor house, do now. We clutched one another's hands and fled past him. He and his family were the only people that we knew who enjoyed every moment of their lives. They were always jesting and laughing. Other people, except for bouts of horse-play, smiled rarely and never laughed. Life to my family, and to all respectable families, was a duty of serious hard work, by which came wealth and respect in this world and in the world to come. The Irishman and his family travelled a great distance every Sunday to a

Roman Catholic church. I have never seen it. I know only that it was a long way off where the people were different from ourselves and, I felt it was inferred, such as it would be undesirable to know.

In my earliest days the schoolmaster went on horseback from farm to farm, staying a day or two at each, and leaving a batch of lessons to be learnt before his next visit. I remember a coloured globe of the world, a prize for my diligence, on which the Arctic and Antarctic and large areas of Africa and South America were blank, except for the words 'Unexplored Interior'.

Although we children were not enthusiasts for learning we could not escape the goad of our elders, to whom education was a passion. When we improved, their faces showed their pleasure. When we fell into lassitude, they showed their pain and debated whether we were sickening for something. We were even threatened with the dreaded molasses drench. This was inflicted upon us once a year, in the first warm spell of spring, a loathsome concoction of many ingredients of which I still taste sour molasses and feel the gritty sulphur between my teeth. I think, too, there was paraffin in this drench which, in anticipation, was so horrible that we wished the spring might never come.

But spring brought also the delights of the maple syrup season when my sister and I were allowed to spend one night in the bush with Ben, while he boiled the sap. Ben was a farm servant and the dearest of all our friends. The sugar bush was miserably cold, with its rotting ice and the dull oxen dragging their sledge with its tank from tree to tree. But inside the sugar shed the oak logs blazed and roared under the vats, and the air was hot and heavy with sweetness. We assured Ben that we would stoke the fires all night while he rested. But soon we climbed into his bunk and lay on the soft buffalo robes. Then Ben, dear Ben, would put another robe on top of us and tuck us in.

II

One of my grandfather's vanities was to own a pair of trotting ponies. We children were allowed to ride them, but they were over-fed and under-exercised and soon threw us off. They would stand while we remounted, and then fling us off again. These ponies were bred for racing. They must always trot, never gallop. My grandfather did not race his ponies, since racing was sinful. It took farmers from their work and brought betting men and whisky drinkers into the neighbourhood. These ponies were vain creatures. As they trotted they lifted their forefeet high and flung them forward. They arched their necks. Their manes and tails streamed in the wind of their flight. Their only duties were to take my grandfather and grandmother to church and to market. Once, when there was a fair in our nearest village, seven miles away, an Indian boy was wagering himself to outrun any pony or pair in a race of two miles or upward. Now, all of the well-off farmers fancied their ponies, yet the Indian boy beat them. He was left far behind at the start but he came back to the fair well in the lead. I learned later that the boy's name was Tom Longboat. He was tall and slim and dark. He was to become Olympic champion at long-distance running.

The working horses on the farm were Clydesdales, big, bony, docile beasts whose lives were calm. On summer evenings each pair that worked together during the day would stand nose to tail, or with necks crossed, under the shelter clump of trees in the grazing field. They stood motionless except for a slow swishing of tails. They did not mind at all when we climbed up by mane or tail and sat on their backs.

The other working animals were a yoke of white oxen. They lived indolent and numb lives. They were interested neither in one another nor in the other cattle. When opportunity came to clear boulders, the heavy yoke was fastened upon their necks and the chains from the yoke were attached to a sledge. The sledge was made of three tree trunks, each some ten inches thick, with a natural upward bend in front.

54

The oxen did the slow jobs of the farm, pulling out stumps, dragging logs and hauling the tank of maple sap. Horses are impatient creatures if baulked at their first attempt. If you set a horse to move a boulder, he would make repeated lunges, and fret himself into hysteria without shifting it. But the oxen, given the word go, simply lay forward on their yoke and pushed. They would hold this position without relaxing or fretting while men levered the boulder out of the ground with crowbars and eased it on to the sledge. During haying and harvest the oxen pushed the long arm of a windlass which raised the trusses and sheaves into the lofts. It was one of my jobs to keep the oxen on the move. Round and round they would go, asleep, so far as I could see, or in a trance. But they were not asleep. A bundle of hay or a sheaf fallen in their way was instantly seized and no shouting or beating would get it from them.

The cattle of our farm were Durhams from which, I believe, the present-day Shorthorn has derived. Except for cheese needed by the household, all of the milk was made into butter. The churning was my job. Sometimes it seemed hours before the thump, thump, in the revolving barrel made known that the butter had formed. Churning was a frenzy of boredom, as was turning the grindstone while one of the men leisurely sharpened axes or mower or binder knives, going frequently into the sunlight to squint at the edge and to test it with a wetted finger, over and over coming back for more grinding. By grandmother's order I had to drink a pint of buttermilk after churning. Buttermilk was almost as horrible as the molasses drench and a mean infliction after the martyrdom of churning.

Swine were many. We called them Yorkshires. Nowadays I think they are known as Large Whites. The swine were never at large except the sows, which had the run of the Old Orchard in summer. Always during the winter and early spring there would be a litter of pigs. We spent hours leaning over the sty wall, looking at a sow stretched on her side while she suckled her squealing babies. The sow grunted with bliss as she suckled them. Suddenly she would get to her feet and nose about in the litter of her sty as though her family had never existed.

Now was the time for the baby pigs to play. They scampered back and forth, snatching mouthfuls of straw and making mock attacks upon one another. They grunted all the while that they played: short, staccato grunts. Then a baby pig would halt suddenly and stare at us from light blue eyes under long blond eyelashes. Then another baby pig would stop and stare. Soon the whole litter would be lined up, staring in silence with quivering snouts. But such inactivity and concentration do not belong to pig childhood, and the baby pigs whirled round to renew their games.

In the end sty the boar lived, a tusked, shaggy, slobbering beast as big as a cow. I used to have nightmares that the boar had broken out of his sty and was chasing me, while I slipped and stumbled. Still, we used to stare at him from a distance, and he in turn stared at us from sunken eyes while he champed his jaws.

An oddity of our farm fifty years ago was a flock of sheep, say a dozen or fifteen of them. Sheep are animals of the open plain. They have no place in a forest country where the snow lies for seven months of the year and may be eight feet deep. This small flock was kept for its wool, which must have been coarse, for the sheep were a shaggy hairy lot. They were small and white, but of no breed that I have ever recognized. In the first pioneer days sheep were needed, for all clothes were made on the farm from the farm's own wool. This little unhappy flock had survived into the days when clothes and rugs and blankets were on sale in our market town, yet the women of our household still spun the wool of our flock and made it into cloth and rugs.

The remaining farm animals were turkeys, geese and fowls. These were cared for by the women and their profit belonged to them. I cannot say by what jugglery of accounting the women were compensated, for there never were sales of poultry or eggs. Probably it was a simple carrying on of a tradition that the women saw to the poultry.

The turkey-cock had six adoring wives. The cock never tired of lowering his wings and spreading his tail while he pirouetted round the hens. His wings thrashed the ground and the vulture-like swellings on his neck became inflamed to crimson. Then he would rush forward, gobble and, for a short while, behave as a sane animal. As fast as his wives laid eggs they were taken from them and set under broody hens. By this deception the turkey hens laid thirty or forty eggs as against their normal dozen. Turkeys are cowardly creatures. Even in the midst of a gobble, if we ran towards him, the cock would deflate and scuttle.

The goose family was of two ganders and four geese. The same deception was practised upon them as upon the turkeys, so that autumn found a large gaggle in possession of the Old Orchard. Unlike the turkeys, which rejected the food offered to them and preferred to spoil the harvest fields, the geese were well content to be fed and never left the Old Orchard.

The master gander had the proprietary instinct very strongly developed. Every man or beast that used the lane alongside the Old Orchard was paced by the gander, from inside the orchard. He spread his wings, stretched his neck flat and forward, and hissed. When the enemy had passed beyond his territory the old gander would clap his wings and shout in triumph. Now, the Old Orchard had delicious apples in it which were banished from the New Orchard, where only those kinds were grown which would keep and could be exported. The apple delights of the Old Orchard were Early Harvest, Harvest Honey, Nannynose, Tolman Sweet, Russet and Snow and others that I do not now recall. My sister and I must have those apples, but what of the gander? Wherever we looked through the fence, there he was, fixing us with a cold, bright blue eye. We ventured it often enough, I keeping the gander at bay with a stick while my sister gathered the apples. Many a nip and buffet the gander dealt me, and many an apple I hurled at him. One day we caught him off his guard. We were in the middle of the orchard before he came rushing upon us at a tangent. As usual, I hurled an apple. It struck him upon the side of the head and he collapsed in a heap. If he were dead, so much the better. We wandered in peace from tree to tree. After a long while the gander got unsteadily to his feet. He shook his head and ruffled his feathers. Then he walked slowly, a broken hero, towards his geese and goslings. He did not attack us again. He shouted defiance and victory no more.

Fowls were many and everywhere, and all of one breed, the barnyard breed. Pedigree cocks and settings of eggs would be bought, but they made no difference. The flock remained the barnyard breed, a basic brown embroidered and patched with red, black, white and speckle. They were cunning and combatant, and big and leggy. Cock battled with cock, and hen pecked hen the whole day through. It was a job for my sister and me to know where their nests were hidden, and to collect the eggs. For a start we knew that there would be no eggs in the fowl-house, which was equipped with the sort of nests that hens ought to like to lay in. We used to find their nests in and under mangers, hollowed out of the hay, tunnelled into the weeds, under the woodpile, anywhere, everywhere. In spite of all our searching we were reconciled to seeing a hen emerge clucking from a stolen nest almost under our feet, followed by a dozen new-hatched chicks.

But what about dogs and cats? There were cats in the barn, wild creatures that fled to hiding-places at sight of any human but Ben, who put out milk for them. Unless he were alone, they would not come for their milk.

And dogs? There were no dogs. My family did not like dogs. Besides, on our sort of farm, a dog would not have paid for his keep.

III

The temperature is at zero, the air motionless. The sun shines brilliantly but yields no heat. The chickadees are flocking in the snow at the kitchen door. They have been abundantly fed on weed seeds from the waste shoot of the threshing-box, but they impudently demand more. These tiny speckled birds, the chickadees, are like our English robins and tits in seeking human company in winter, but they are even more cheeky.

The men have fed and cleaned the animals and are shaved and in their best clothes. My grandfather wears a frock coat, my father and uncles morning coats and striped trousers. They sit in the kitchen and living room, awkward and uncomfortable at having nothing to do. On any other fine winter morning of the week they would be fetching wood from the bush and splitting it for the stoves and the furnace. They might be dynamiting stumps or prising out boulders. Or they might be milling flour, or crushing maize or oats, or taking a sleighload of corn to the station.

The women have been baking all morning. Now they have gone upstairs to dress. They have come down in their Sunday best, long skirts with bustles, sleeves with puffed shoulders, and hats with birds' feathers.

It is time to leave for church. The women put on fur coats. My mother's is of beaver. The men wear coats of bear fur which double their girth, with caps of musk-rat fur to cover their ears. Everyone wears fur mittens. Ben is at the gate, holding the ponies' heads. They are dancing about and whinnying, for they love this cold, dry, sunny weather. My grandfather and grandmother get into the front of the sleigh, and I wedge myself between them. My father and mother are in the back seat, my sister between them, more comfortable than I, for my grandfather is a very large man. We shuffle our feet into the straw which litters the bottom of the sleigh. My grandfather takes the reins. Ben tucks buffalo robes round our legs. The ponies are frantic now, but my grandfather holds them firmly. We can feel the old man's pride. Then he eases the reins and the ponies dash forward, breaking into a gallop until the bit brings them to a trot. The going is perfect, for the snow has been packed as hard as ice. The runners of the sleigh sing as we sway from side to side or bump across the hollows in the road surface.

The rest of the family follow in a bobsleigh, a sort of wagon on runners which will carry a dozen passengers. The bobsleigh is drawn at a slow trot by the working horses, and we children are very conscious of the superior style of our horses and conveyance.

There is a long shed at the church for the shelter of the horses. My father unhitches our team and halters them to the manger. He pours out a sack of mixed hay and chaff for them. Then he throws our buffalo robes over their backs and buckles them under their bellies.

By the time the service has ended, and it seems to take hours, my sister and I are hungry. We do not know what time it is, but only that we are hungry. The men form one group outside the church and the women another. We children make a faint attempt to group and converse in imitation, but soon we disperse and cling to our elders' hands. They talk and they talk. We squirm, but they go on talking. We are too young to realize that this is the club of the grown-ups, their one opportunity to exchange news and views, to express themselves, to get out of and away from themselves.

But at last a family hitches team to sleigh and starts for home after many good-byes and so-longs, using Christian names now, so-long James, so-long Alf. Soon all have left. Although I am so hungry I fall asleep. When my overcoat, jersey, cap and mittens are taken off I am still more sleepy than hungry. But the smell of food revives me. We have roast beef, potatoes, parsnip, squash. Then suet pudding. Then pumpkin pie covered in cream.

On Sunday afternoons we children might go for a walk, but we must not play. We might read, but the reading must be approved by our elders. The Bible was preferred, but *Paradise Lost*, Livingstone's *Missionary Travels* and *Pilgrim's Progress* were tolerated.

After our Sunday high tea we gathered in the sitting-room, which was very warm, far warmer than we would like in England. The windows were double, with an air space of six inches between them. All doors to the outside were double too, with a yard of space between them.

It is the turn now for my father or one of my uncles to read from the Bible. When that is ended the boy from Barnardo's Homes is sent to bed. Ben, too, came from Barnardo's Homes but stayed with the farm for many years and became one of the family. My earliest memory is riding upon his shoulder, with the snow piled on either side higher than my head. He was a slight quiet man of refined features, very unlike my burly relations. We children loved him for his gentleness and patience. He looked more a clerk than a farm labourer. He was, for example, clean-shaven, whereas my father and uncles were heavily moustached and my grandfather wore a great square beard.

There might be desultory talk for a while between the men about the business of the farm while the women sewed and gossiped in whispers. On a Sabbath evening the stimulus to conversation of cider, wine and raspberry cordial was forbidden. Raspberry cordial was the favourite tipple of the women. My grandmother by now would be placidly asleep in her chair. Ben would be reading *Pilgrim's Progress* to my sister and me, she on his knee while I crouched at his feet. Ben knew how to leave out the sermon parts and read us only the adventures. One of my uncles, who held strong political views, might try to get an argument going, but no one save himself cared a button for politics. Still, his practice on us got him into the Canadian Parliament later on. Soon my sister would be very sleepy and go to bed. Then my father would play hymns on the piano. Unhappily this always provoked my non-political uncle to an accompaniment on the fiddle. No one has ever played the fiddle so badly or so excruciatingly slightly out of tune. The company would hum the hymns quietly. My mother would say to me: 'Your sister has been in bed an hour, hadn't you better go to bed too?' But I would beg to be allowed to go with Ben on the late night rounds of the barn. We did not put on coats or caps or mittens. Our store of warmth was enough to take us to the barn. There it would be warm as in the house, because of the fermentation of the silage and hay. In the intense cold

61

outside the stars hung very near to the earth, with sharp spears of blue shooting from them. Perhaps the Northern Lights would be playing, creeping up from the horizon to where we stood, in thick curtains of blue, green, white and orange. Then they would vanish and appear again as an immense arch of blue and orange.

The barn, by the light of our hurricane lamps, was vast, mysterious and silent, reminding me of the cathedral in Toronto I had visited once at evening time. We went downstairs to the warmth and sweet smell of the cattle. There were the two lines of cows, most of them lying down and all chewing the cud. To our left was the pen of calves. Beyond the calves, the pigs. To our right was the large pen of store cattle, all of them lying at rest in the straw. The turkeys had a pen beyond the store cattle. As the light approached they began to mutter, and fidgeted on their perches. Next to the turkeys were the fowls, some of them, for most of them were perched in the barn above, or on the cattle mangers, or anywhere but in their quarters. The bull regarded us moodily from his isolated cell. He was standing, and Ben rubbed his hand for a while over his forehead and muzzle. Then we went to the horses. They were all wide awake. They whinnied as we came in. Ben patted each one. If some were patted and some not you might have trouble with sulks in the morning. Then Ben opened the stable door and held his lantern high to see the sheep. Their low wall was topped by iron bars to the roof, for sheep would be a most desirable meal for the grey wolves. As the light fell upon them they flocked in a mass to a corner, and then, by a sudden impulse, flocked to another corner.

All was well. We went past the pigs on our way outward to the stairs. Some of the sows got to their feet and came to the front of their sties. These Ben scratched hard with his fingers and the sows grunted with pleasure.

We must have been a long while in the barn, for my mother said severely: 'Now you really must go to bed, look at the time.' My father, who never ordered me to do anything, smiled at me in a man-to-man understanding that it was useless to argue with a woman.

So I bade good night and fled up the cold stairs to the warmth of my tiny bedroom. I opened the curtains and the stars poured their piercing light through the window. Then I took off my shoes and socks and dug my toes in the fur of the black bear skin which lay beside my cot. The skin gave off a musky smell. Suddenly I was very tired and sleepy. I could hear, as in a dream, the grey wolves howling to one another, desolate terrible cries as of creatures damned, first from in front of the house, then from behind.

We children always enjoyed our Sundays. There were tedious spells during the day, but the evenings were the most pleasant of the week. We were allowed to stay up late and listen to our elders who, on every other evening, were dispersed and alone, each at his own task or hobby. On Sunday evenings they must be together, for their religion forbade any but the essential tasks of feeding themselves and their animals. They might read or sew, for these were improving employments. 'Is it not as improving to make furniture as to make rugs?' I would ask. My grandfather explained in many words which carried to me not the least conviction or satisfaction.

I was fast asleep when my mother came to bid me a last good night.